oatn and agave

a poememe parody

notta poette

(a poetic parody of
"milk and honey" by rupi kaur
and modern 'instagram'-style poetry)

gifted from Beth + Duncan Shelton for my 24th Birthday.

copyright © 2020 by Notta Poette

FIRST EDITION

all rights reserved. no part of this book may be reproduced or used in any manner without written permission of the copyright owner except for the use of quotations in a book review.

contents

foreword
dear rupi

the meme-ing

the "misandry"

the crying tbh

the good vibez

foreword

i write these words
for the people who can
(or for those who hope to)
laugh at their darkness

for the people
who share my heart

for my comrades

for the people i have been
and the people i will be

and most of all,
for the friends and fans of the page
who were there for me in good times and bad,
and who made all of this possible
through their kind and generous support -

i am so deeply grateful to you all, for it all :
for being a family to me when i had none, for the laughs we
share, the growth we encourage in each other, the quiet and the
loud understandings, the inside jokes, the tender moments, the
big moods, the real sense of community, and for all of the life-
long bonds that started off in comment threads

to be able to share
my silly poememes, my art, and my internet life
with you
is truly my greatest honor

thank you so, so, SO much

i love you

dear rupi,

you are an inspiring woman
and an iconic poet

thank you for
reviving a passion for words
in the modern age,
for knowing the power of vulnerability,
and for not being afraid
to speak up and speak out

your body of work
is beautiful, heartwrenching, strong, impactful, wise -
and through it, you have changed the lives of many
for the better, including my own

i hope this parody
of your world-changing first book
makes you smile, and feel, and laugh

thank you for bringing poetry
to the social media era

thank you for all the ways
you continue to create and share
the beauty of your heart and mind

and

thank you for being
so meme-able

the meme-ing

destroy me,
my love:

as if i were
a popular rap song

and you,
a white girl
with a
ukulele

maybe
she's
born with it -

maybe it's
trauma-related
coping mechanisms

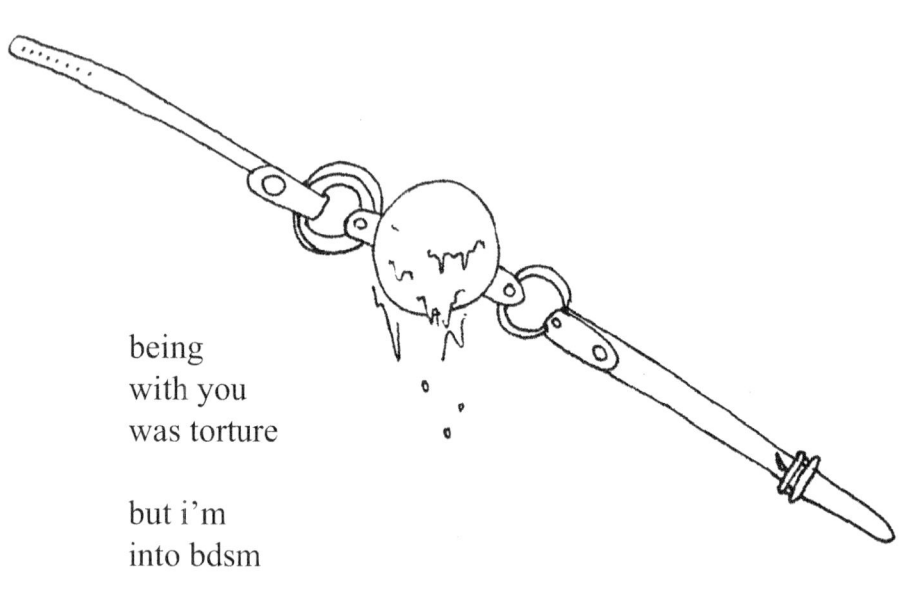

being
with you
was torture

but i'm
into bdsm

you said,
'there is
no greater passion.
my darling,
than mine
for you

you are the
only one for me

i would die
a thousand deaths
for you, my love'

and
i did
finger guns

because
how the fuck
do you
respond to that

they say that
every seven years,
you have a new body

fifty trillion cells
live and die in each of us -
a silent, constant rebirth

i hope
this is the case:

for soon,
i will have
a body
that has
never worn
a naruto headband

sorry about
what i said
when i was
drunk

i meant it,
but i
didn't
want you
to know

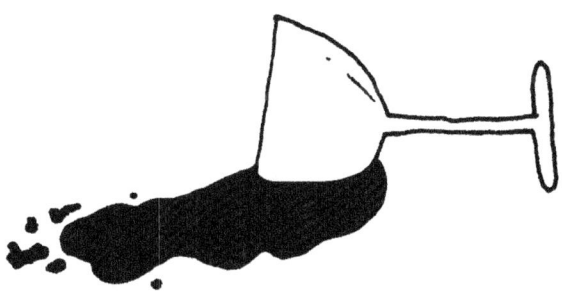

our love
felt cute
but
you
deleted it later

he wanted to
steal her heart
but she was
too busy
stealing from
walmart

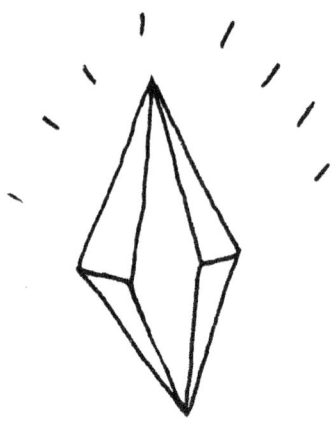

i thought
i was
your
favorite
sim
but you
took out
my stairs
when i
went for
a swim

her
milkshake
brought
all the boys
to the yard

but
she was
gay

she was the core
of the world;

magnetic
and iron
and burning hot
as a star -

he was
a flat earther

sometimes
i think i
do too many drugs
but sometimes
i think i
don't do enough

you had
the kind of love
i had to
ask reddit
for advice about

i wasn't
born
for "doing math" -
i was born
to Perform, darling

roses
are red
violets
are blue -
sometimes
you don't think it
be like it is
but it do

he was
an easily
preventable disease

she was
an anti-vax child

i will never
love you
as much as
my cats
and you just
have to live
with that

you said
you wanted me
but you
were bluffing

i shaved my
goddamn legs
for nothing

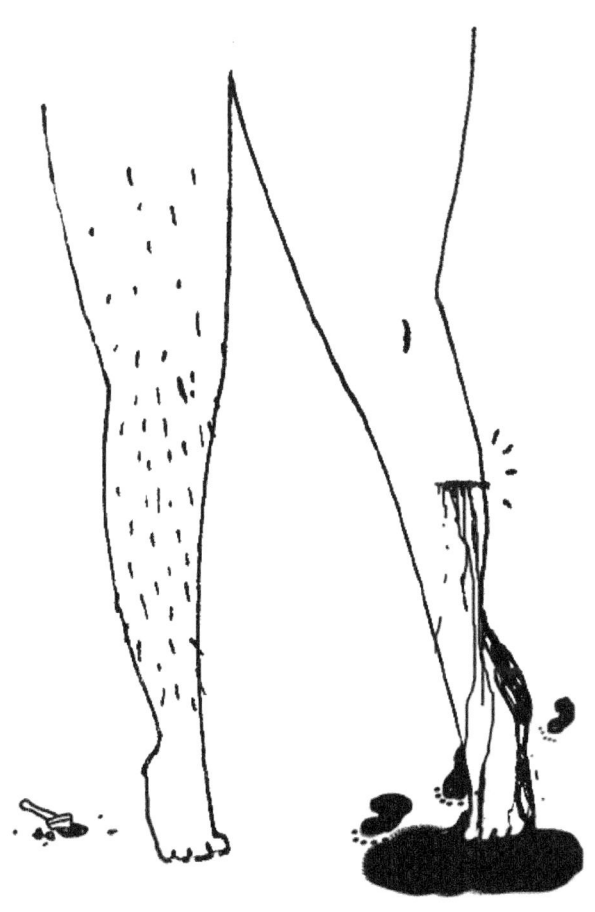

being with you
was a
music festival:

i was
high
the whole time

yeah i'll
fucking cry
over spilt milk
do you know
how expensive milk is

who,
me?

i don't
know her

i got
ninety-nine problems
and
they're all
capitalism

i am not only
slightly lapsing
into madness

i am
speed running
this bitch

if you
say something
and i say
"what"

and you say
"never mind,
it's nothing"

and i say
"what is it"

and you say
"nothing,
forget about it"

just know
that i will
never ever
forget about it

and i'll be
thinking about it
on my deathbed

infect me
with
your love,
darling -

as if
i were
the family
computer
in 2002

and you,
the
limewire file
linking_park_numb_real_mp3.exe

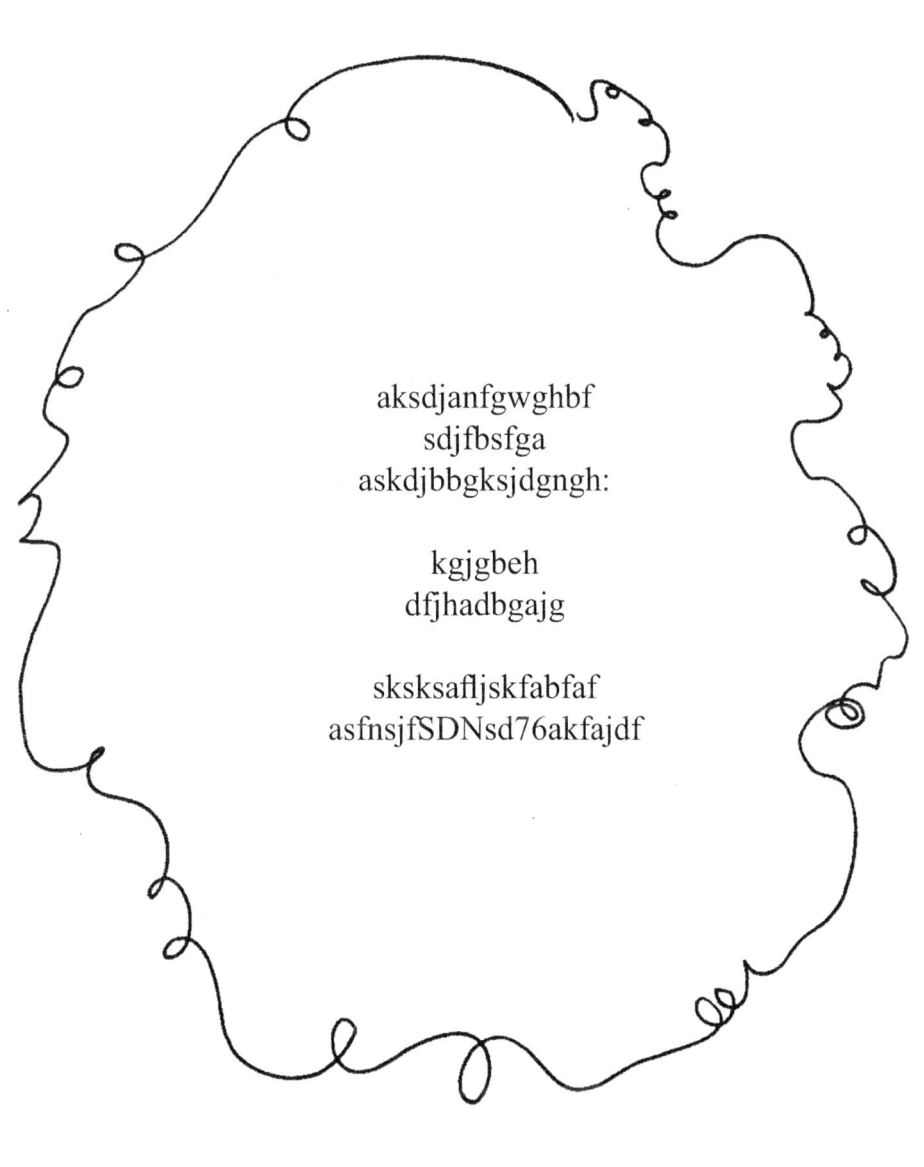

i'm just
a girl,
standing in front
of a girl,
asking her
if she
has seen
any of my hair elastics anywhere like there must be ONE
around somewhere right we just bought
like a shit ton what the fuck where are they

home
is where
it smells
like weed

he said
'i love you'

she said
'ok boomer'

i may
be cringe
but i am
free

i saw you
everywhere

as if you were
that pattern
from the
bus seats

he
was an
insomniac

she
was a
vine compilation

but what if
life is nothing but
an endless scroll
through netflix,
desperately looking
for something to watch
and you finish
your food
before you decide?

i'm braver
than i
think i am

(unless
there's
a spider)

i think of you
and a garden
blooms inside me

i walk among
the rows of blossoms
and run my
soft fingertips along them

all of the
flowers are poisonous

hell yeah

i do a line
of the nectar

she was
the wind in
his undercut,
his three am
"u up" text

he was her
wish brand
kylie jenner
lip kit dupe

the vibes
weren't "off"
but they
most certainly
weren't "on"

being
with you
is like an episode
of riverdale
because
what the fuck is going on

i went through
deeply fucked up trauma
and all i got
was this
undervalued genius

the only thing
worse than my
hand-eye coordination
is my
heart-brain coordination

wow i'd love to
but i literally
would hate it
so i won't

as we floated there,
in the cold and
endless dark
of the atlantic,
titantic debris
sinking all around us

you screamed
my name
and said you'd
never
let me go -

but you
also didn't
invite me up on the
shipwreck debris
with you

and
there was
totally room for me
up there

so
i'm, like,
kind of getting
mixed signals

the "misandry"

i apologize,
good sir;
i did not
realize
i had to
cover my soft hands
in bubble wrap
before
handling
your masculinity

i wish
some m*n had
a personality
instead
of a
beard

she was
a high school
free from
gun violence

he was
an entitled
white guy

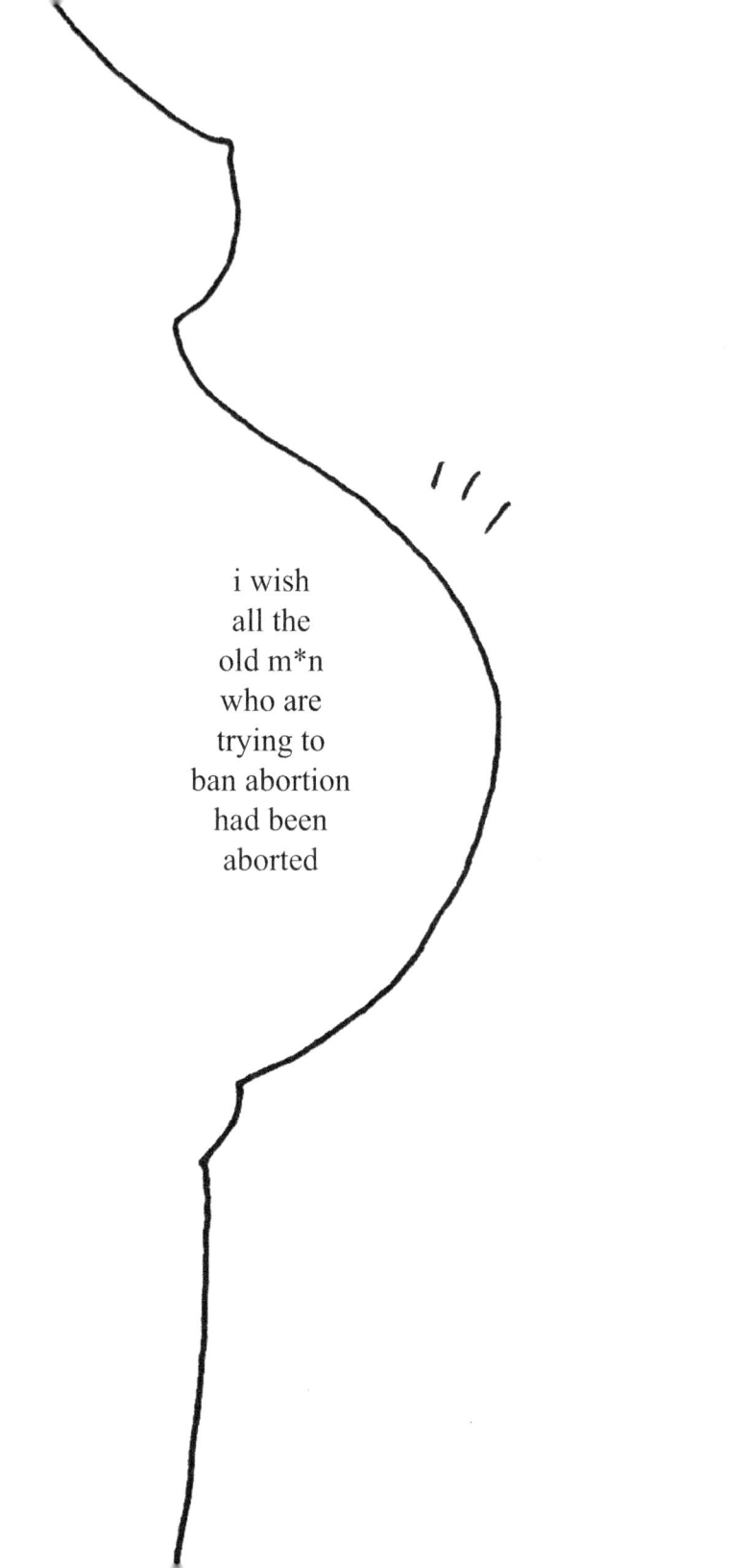

i wish
all the
old m*n
who are
trying to
ban abortion
had been
aborted

waste your
own damn time
you don't
need a m*n
to do that for you

i do not owe
strange m*n
my kindness

i do not care
if you thought
my tone to be
"not very nice"

i do not have to
please you
and be cordial
because you want me
to please you and be cordial

i do not have to
"smile"

i don't have to
make you
feel comfortable
while you make me
uncomfortable

listen,
i'm not
saying
'all m*n'

but i am
definitely
not saying
'not all m*n'

you think
the friendzone
is bad?

imagine
thinking
someone
was your
friend

and the
whole time
they were
only trying
to fuck you

crazy how
women saying
"please don't
rape and kill us"
is still
so controversial

if you're
coming to ME
for boyfriend advice??

you already
want to
break up with him,
girl

K

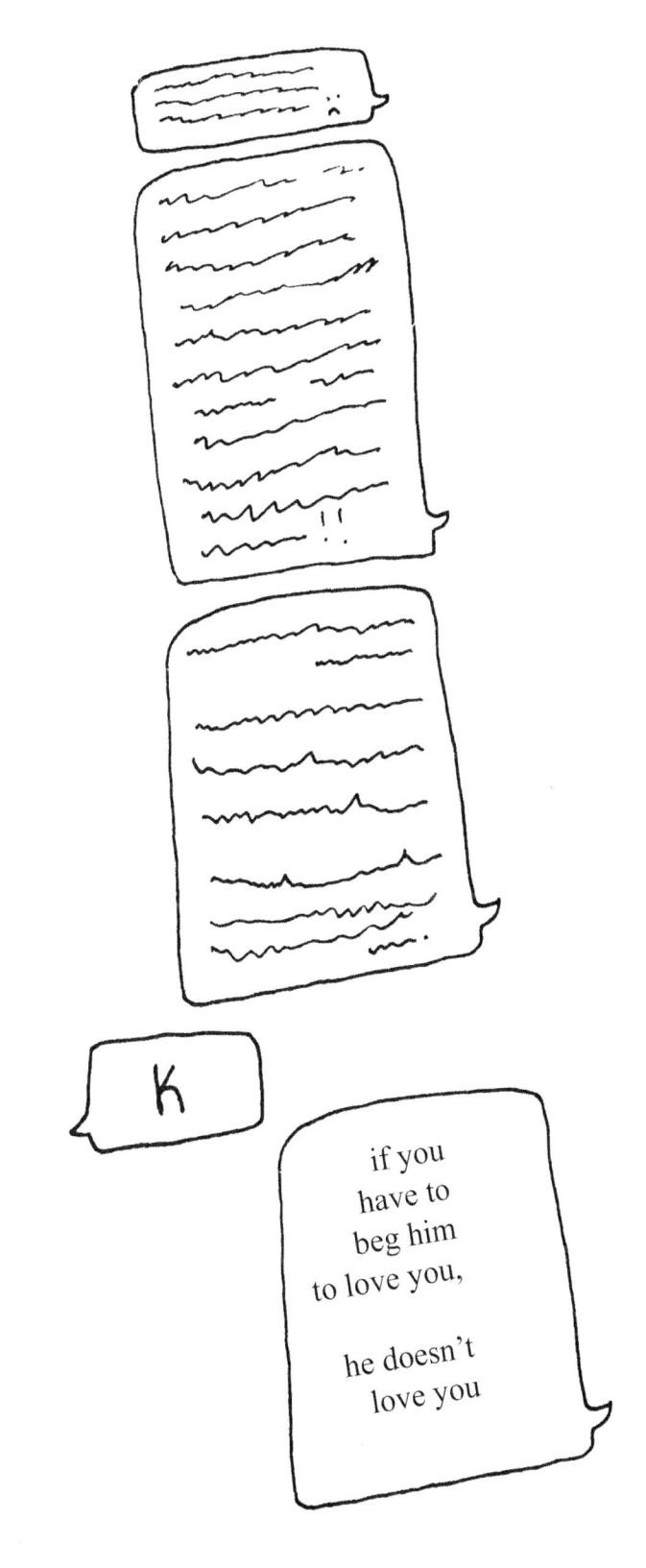

if you
have to
beg him
to love you,

he doesn't
love you

every day
women are
spoken for by m*n -

even the most
powerful among us
are not free

we are forced
to smile, to dance, to sing
for them -
we are forced to
obey them

we are only allowed
the happiness
of a domesticated animal -

and we are
reminded
every day
what happens
if we bite

m*n make up
all kinds of
pathetic, desperate games
for themselves
to figure out
"what women want"
instead of
just listening
to women

every day
every woman
has multiple events
occur to her
that would be
her joker moment
if we were
as fragile
as m*n are

i wasn't
always
a m * n hating feminist

what a
waste of time
that was

m*n aren't
actually funny
we're just afraid
they'll kill us
if we don't laugh

ah yes,
the "extreme feminists" -
you know, the ones
bombing Hooters
and driving their cars
into hockey stands
full of m*n?

the "extreme feminists",
hanging out on 4chan
and planning school shootings
because of "misandry"

the "extreme feminists",
taking power in government
and writing legislature
that tells m*n what to do
with their bodies

ah, yes,
the "extreme feminists" -
the reason
m*n walk home at night
with their housekeys
tucked between their fingers

isn't it like
soooo weird
how your
sexist boyfriend
started treating you
exactly like
all of his "crazy exes"
the minute you
didn't exist
to please him?

"what do
you mean,
toxic
masculinity?

are you
saying
i'm toxic,
bitch?"

he screamed,
punching through
the wall

you have to
care about women
when they are
not in the room

you have to
care about women
who weren't born
with a womb

 you have to
care about women
you're not attracted to

you have to
care about women
even when it's hard to do

i *wish*
you could
be sexist
to m*n

women
are never
more "ugly"

than after
they turn
down a m*n

who,
moments ago,

wanted to
fuck them

jolene,
PLEASE take
my m*n

feminism
is only
a scary word

if you're worried
that women
will start
treating you

the way
you
treat women

boys being
mean to you
isn't hot
love yourself

sometimes i
look back
at gullible,
fresh young me
and then
at all of
the adult m*n
who surrounded her
like vultures to a corpse
and i still
tremble

m*n are
violent
and deny
their violence
because they didn't
even notice
it occurred

ok buddy, sure;
not all m*n

but
some of them,
right?

you acknowledge
some m*n are
indeed the way
you claim to oppose,
right?

so then,
can you
point out
which among
your friends
is one of them?

because
i promise -
the women in your life
certainly could

m*n
are
cancelled

reminder that
our bodies
are not
your incubators,
your fleshlights,
your punching bags,
your blow up sex dolls,
your target practice,
or your property

if you say
you can't be
in a room
alone
with a woman
for fear of
being accused
of rape -
you're telling
on yourself

a m*n
walks into
my field of vision

i pretend
i do not see it

i am trying
to forgive myself
for the things i did
when i thought
my value
was measured
by m*n

if your idea
of "masculinity"
is anger and repression -
that's fucking
sad

if your idea
of "masculinity"
allows for no weakness -
that's fucking
weak

live,
laugh,
leave him

the crying tbh

you swore
you would
never
yeet me

so
why is
this bitch
so empty

i think
of you
and
i suffer
like a cat

starving
to death
with
the bowl
still half full

mow

how
dare you
talk
about me
the way
i talk
about
myself

don't ask me
how i am

i'm not
good

you don't
tag me
in memes
anymore

sorry for

ghosting you

i was

dissociating

not sure
if you're
the trauma
or the
coping mechanism

i thought
i was
being very clear
but no one
understood me

i wish
i knew
more about
my childhood
but i know
my brain
forgot
for a reason

you fucked me up
beyond repair,
darling -

as if
i were
mother earth,

and you;

capitalism

every picture
we took
together
was a
cursed image

sometimes,
even the artists
meet a sadness
they can't
make beautiful

it is
just sadness

there is nothing
beautiful
about it

time flies
when you
thought
you would
be dead
by twenty

when you
ghosted me,
it hurt enough -

why did
you have
haunt me,
too?

my heart
is
a bus -

always
too full

and

always
too late

next time
could you
stab me
in the
front?

i grow tired
of all these
"petit morts"

when do i get
the big one

heartbreak
happens twice:

the first,
when you remove
the emojis
from their contact info

the second,
when netflix tells you
that they watched
an episode of your show
                        without you

sometimes
i worry
that we're just
staying together
for the
cats

the
safe word
is
"commitment"

arizona iced tea
was one dollar, once

there was a time when
you were a good person, once

those days are
long dead, now

and i took them all
for granted

so what
if i still
think about you?

i promise -
it's not
fondly

i almost
thought that
i was
missing you
for a second
but
i was just
sober

there is not much
i wouldn't do
to make you
happy

but i won't
make myself
unhappy

time
heals
all
wounds

except for
the ones
it makes
worse

you
were
lipgloss
on the
windiest day
of my life

i get that
you're a gamer
but
stop playing
with my heart

if i never
ever ever
ever ever
ever ever
ever ever
ever ever
ever ever
ever ever
ever ever
ever ever
ever ever
ever ever
ever ever
ever ever
ever ever
ever ever
ever ever
ever ever
see you again -

it will be
too soon

i miss you
but
we live
in the same house

sorry
i'm late

i was
crying

i gave you
the best of me
and you
didn't want it

today i saw a human
that i used to
laugh and cry and dance with
in line at the coffeeshop -

(a person who used to tell me
what the texture of their dreams were,

what the darkness
in their soul sounds like,

what their fears and
hopes and joys were,

a human i used to spend 2 ams with,
wine drunk on the kitchen floor) -

and we
awkwardly talked
about the weather

(a sad note from the author:
as i edit this book,
it strikes and stills me
to realize that
it seems
i have forgotten
who this poem
was even about)

thank god
we
never
got those
matching tattoos

was my
heart
just cartilage -
and you,
a piercing gun
at claires?

sometimes
bad things
happen
and
there is
no reason
for them

sometimes
there is not
even a lesson
to be learned

sometimes
it just hurts

sometimes
you just scar

unblock me
you coward

how
do i
delete my
life account

bye 5ever lol

i truly believe
you're not
a bad person
i just wish
you were
good to me

can't
believe
i made
a playlist
for you

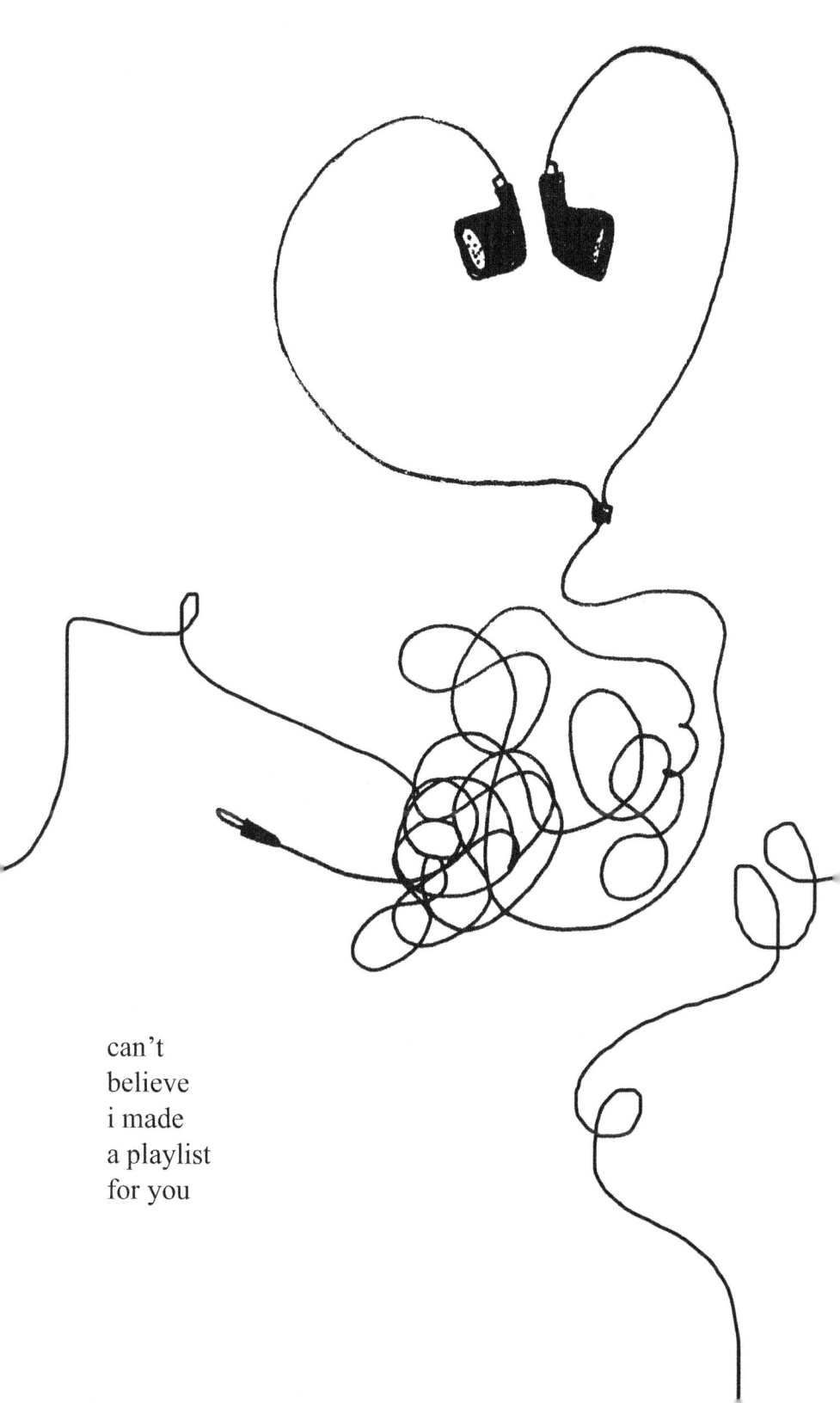

darling
i love you
but
please
get your shit together

we could have
a beautiful friendship
if we both weren't
too depressed
to leave
our houses

i made
some of
the best memories
i'll ever forget
with you

i guess
some people
choose to
hate you

for the
things
they did
to you

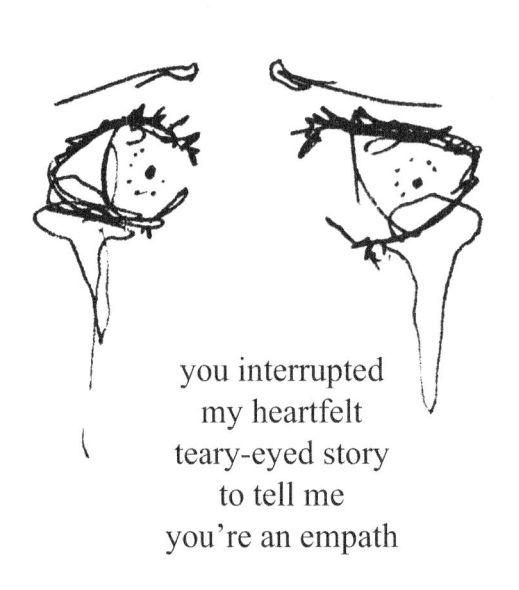

you interrupted
my heartfelt
teary-eyed story
to tell me
you're an empath

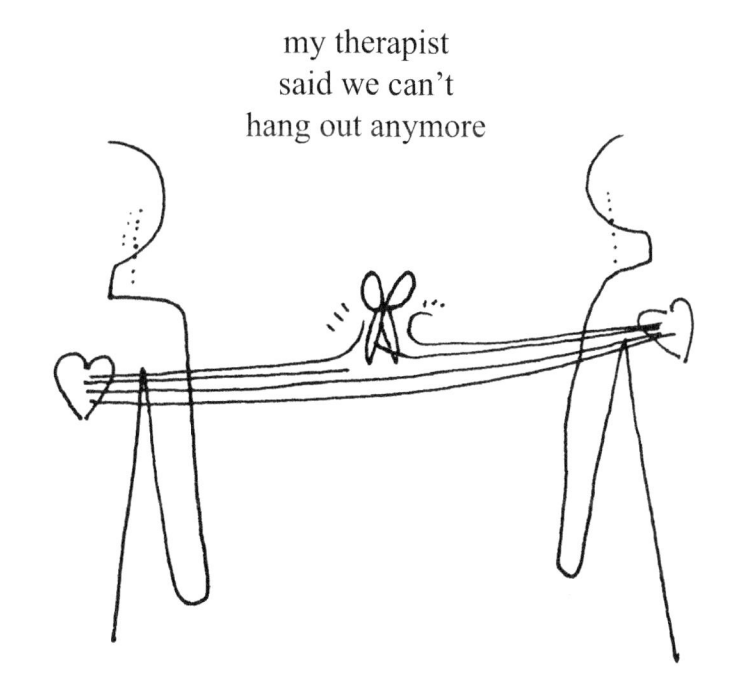

my therapist
said we can't
hang out anymore

i understand
why you're like this
but fuck i wish
you weren't like this

i just want
to feel loved
without
asking for it

you rolled over
in our shared bed
'cause it was too hot
and i took it personally

how do i
even begin
to explain this
to my therapist

for
financial reasons,
i will be
dying

i am at war
with my body

it is dying
and yet, i decorate
as if i just moved in

my trauma
did not
make me funny

i made me
funny
against all odds
and in spite of
traumatic experiences
that tried to kill me

the thought of death
did not teach me to laugh

i taught myself
to laugh at death

i reach out
to those
who have
long ago
abandoned me

i hurt anew
when they
subsist the silence

i wish
they knew
what they did to me

i wish
they knew
what i had to
survive
without them

all the songs
you wrote
about me
were in
a minor key

for
someone with
no rhythm
you sure
know how
to dance around
the subject

if you could
start being
more consistent
with how you treat me
that would be great
because my
spotify algothrim
is having a panic attack

you
left me
to die
like
i was your
neopet

perhaps
you thought
my texts
were
terms and conditions
because
you never
read them

was the
sex good
or was it
the only time
my brain
got dopamine
while in
your presence

you let me down
more than
the public education system

i love
like i pour
laundry detergent:

probably too much

i wish i
could delete
other people's
memories of me

comfort
is a dress
i never have
the occasion to wear

some people
will think of you
a cruelty
for clearly stating
your needs and boundaries

like spring,
coming every year
even after
the frost and decay -
i apologize
to you
for the hurt
you gave
to me

alexa,
play me
the last
message
where
their voice
still sounded
like they
loved
me

my trauma
stole all
of my youth

and with it;

my gentleness
to myself,

my memories
of the farbetween Good Times
(few as they were),

my willingness
to trust,

and probably
my ability
to do math
like i swear
i used to be
like
really good
at math

*"no one will ever
love you like i do!"*

they screamed at me,
slicing their calloused skin
on their own
freezing-hot barbed-wire rage

trembling as i gathered up
what little was 'mine' in the world,
they stood, frenzied, over me -
wild-eyed and rabid -
and repeated those words
over and over and over
like a curse, like a prayer,
like a mantra, like a promise:

*"no one will ever
love you like i do
no one will ever
love you like i do
no one will ever love you like i do no one will ever
love you like i do no one will ever love you like i
do"*

not
realizing
that

that was
the point

i wish
i was
a part of
my family

life hack:
give up

i love you
but i don't
like-like you

i wonder
what i wasted
more precious time on :

missing you?

or looking
for my vape?

i killed
a fake plant

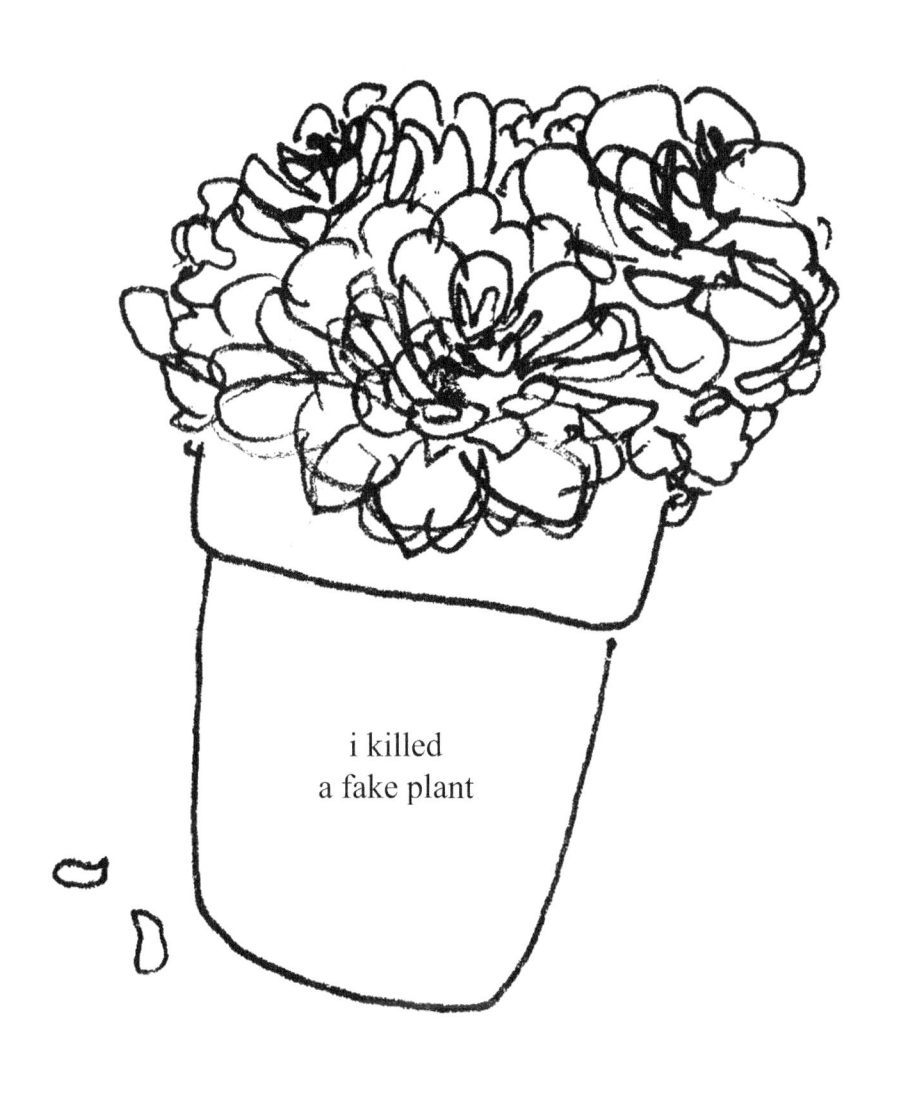

the good vibez

you ever
just turn
your head
and kiss
your own
shoulder
and be
like
'luv u'?

if past you
isn't cringe
you didn't
grow

sometimes
you just
have to
put on
some clothes
and make
some coffee
and blast
some abba
and
pretend
to be
a functional
human being
until you
believe it

you should've
missed me
when i
missed you back

maybe,
that's how
our story
goes:

you -
the crack
on the
sidewalk,
the rain
on the cacti,
the synapse
and
symphony,
the quiet
hand of fate

and me -
unable to
stop singing
'all star'
whenever there's
a lull in
conversation

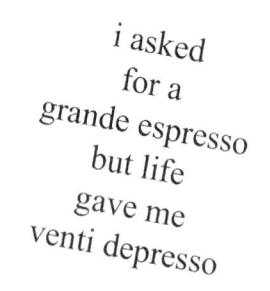

i asked
for a
grande espresso
but life
gave me
venti depresso

thank you,
corner store dude,
for never judging me
to my face

can someone
who knows astrology
please tell me
what is wrong with me

please
forgive me
daddy marx
but
i need
to order something
from amazon

if you leave
me on read...
that is
totally fine i know you are busy and will
get back to me when you have a sec i love you

y'all mind if i
love myself
even though
i'm not perfect
because i know
i do my best
to be kind to others
and i deserve
that kindness too???

i already saw
the meme
but i pretend
to laugh
because
i love you

despite it all,
i want
to trust
the universe

with no
evidence,
i believe
that believing
is enough

it is
the best
we can do ;

indeed,
it is
all
we can do

if spite
is all you have
to get you up
in the morning -

it's enough

i only
wear bras
if they will be
removed passionately
by a lover
within the hour

that was
the last time
i will miss
a night out
with my friends
due to crying
over you

i don't
give a fuck
if you don't
like me
but i need
to know
precisely why

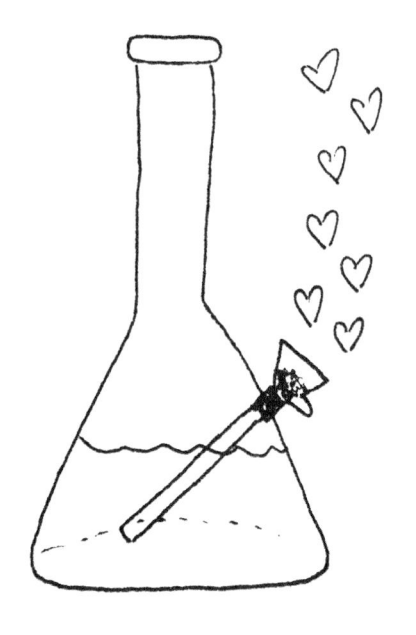

weed

pretending
to be strong
is still
being strong

you're not
really pretending

you're out there,
doing it anyway

that's strength

had a
nightmare
that i
gave
a fuck

double text

go to
the party

make
the art

use the
good soap

tell them
how you feel

cry when
you need to

draw on
your bus ticket

laugh loud
in quiet rooms

wear the
ugly sweater

who cares

life is an abyss
unless you give it
meaning

i hope
all the girls
i met in
bar bathrooms
at 2am
are having
a good day

yes i use
'she' pronouns
but
like how
a level 5 hurricane
is also
a "she"

i've already
repressed
this moment
goodbye

i am allowed
joy,
even if i have
made mistakes

i am allowed
to offer myself
kindness

i am allowed
to feel loved

i am allowed
to be soft
to the sharpest parts of me

i am allowed
to allow myself space
to allow myself
to create a space for me

bad people
don't worry
about being
bad people

ceci
n'est pas
une poememe

i'm so glad
we're happy
and i'm not
just stuck here
'cause of rent

i want a love
so bold
and true
and explicit
that
the historians
won't ever
be able to say
we were
just
roommates

my
tarot cards
told me
you're
a bitch

damn
you still
hate me??

that's wild
because
i don't
think about
you
at all

loving you
is like
doing
peace signs

i just
can't
stop

ummm
you should
be nicer
to me

i am
a poet

and if
you keep
this up

i'll have
to write
another book

i think
of love
and
i notice
like a cat

starving
to death
with
the bowl
still half full

m o w

it's okay
if you are
the only person
who believes
in you
at first:

others
will join you
sooner
than you think

♡

Printed in Great Britain
by Amazon